new apartment design

daab

Este libro refleja algunas de las últimas tendencias en el diseño de interiores. Innovadores arquitectos y diseñadores de todo el mundo proyectan una original visión de los espacios, teniendo como únicos límites las paredes maestras y la imaginación. New Apartment Design está destinado a aquellas personas dispuestas a transformar su vivienda en un espacio personal, disfrutando de sensaciones, colores, formas y texturas que son la imagen del estilo y de la propia personalidad. La luz recupera el protagonismo y define la estructuración de los espacios y su decoración. Junto con la madera y otros materiales naturales se buscan sensaciones táctiles y visuales perdidas en las ciudades, pero sin renunciar a los gustos y a las necesidades urbanas.

Ce livre reflète certaines des dernières tendances du design d'intérieur. Des architectes novateurs et des designers du monde entier y projettent une vision originale des espaces, n'ayant comme limites que les murs porteurs et l'imagination. New Apartment Design est destiné aux personnes prêtes à transformer leur intérieur en un espace personnel, par un jeu de sensations, de couleurs, de formes et de textures à l'image de leur style et de leur personnalité. La lumière joue un rôle essentiel dans la définition et la structuration des espaces et dans leur décoration. Grâce au bois et aux matériaux naturels, on retrouve des sensations tactiles et visuelles absentes des villes, sans toutefois renoncer au caractère et aux besoins citadins.

Questo libro riflette alcune delle ultime tendenze nella progettazione d'interni. Audaci architetti e progettisti di tutto il mondo creano un'originale visione degli spazi, mantenendo come uniche limitazioni i muri portanti e l'immaginazione. New Apartment Design è destinato a chi è disposto a trasformare la casa in uno spazio personale, gustando sensazioni, colori, forme e texture che sono l'immagine dello stile e della propria personalità. La luce recupera protagonismo e definisce l'organizzazione degli spazi e dell'arredamento. Con ill legno ed altri materiali naturali si sono cercate sensazioni tattili e visuali ormai perse nelle città, però senza rinunciare al gusto ed alle necessità urbane.

In diesem Buch sind die neuesten Tendenzen auf dem Gebiet der Innenraumgestaltung vereint. Innovative Innenarchitekten und Designer aus aller Welt zeigen, wie man auf originelle Weise mit dem Raum umgehen kann. Sie lassen ihrer Fantasie freien Lauf und respektieren nur die tragenden Wände. New Apartment Design ist für alle, die ihre Wohnung nach persönlichen Maßstäben umgestalten und dabei mit Empfindungen, Farben, Formen und Texturen ihren persönlichen Stil zum Ausdruck bringen wollen. Eine wichtige Rolle bei der Gestaltung und der Ausschmückung der Innenräume spielt das Licht. Daneben sollen durch Einsatz von Holz und anderen natürlichen Materialien in den Städten schon verloren geglaubte Sinneseindrücke wieder belebt werden, ohne jedoch auf die Annehmlichkeiten und Erfordernisse des urbanen Lebens zu verzichten.

This book embodies some of the latest trends in interior design, displaying the work of innovative architects from around the world, who project a unique vision of interior spaces limited only by the extent of their imagination. New Apartment Design is intended for those who wish to transform their home into a personalized space in which to experience sensations, colors, forms and textures that reflect a contemporary aesthetic and the personality of its inhabitant. Light becomes the primary element, defining the distribution and decoration of a given space, along with wood and other materials that search for visual and tactile sensations uncommon to the city, without renouncing the styles and needs that characterize the urban context.

Alberto Natali Architetto | Montecatini Terme, Italy
Apartment in Monsummano Terme
Monsummano Terme | 2003

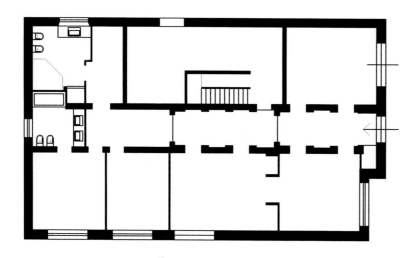

Cha Innerhofer Architecture + Design | New York, USA
Green Penthouse Loft
New York, USA | 2003

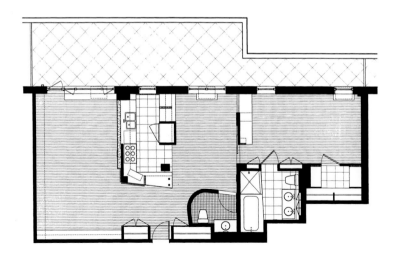

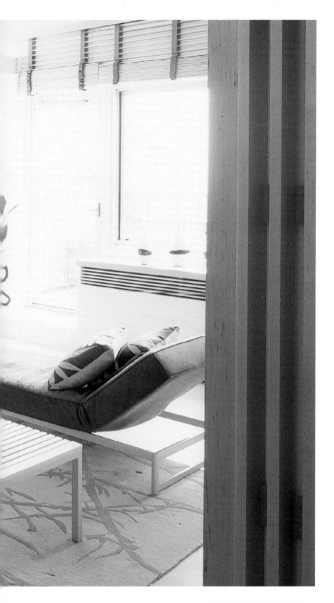

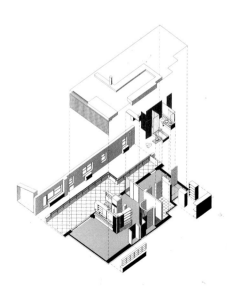

Daniele di Monte | Miami, USA
Apartment in Miami
Miami, USA | 2002

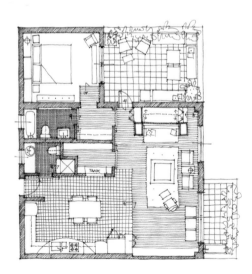

Ellen Rapelius & Xavier Franquesa | Barcelona, Spain
Apartment in Sitges St.
Barcelona, Spain | 2003

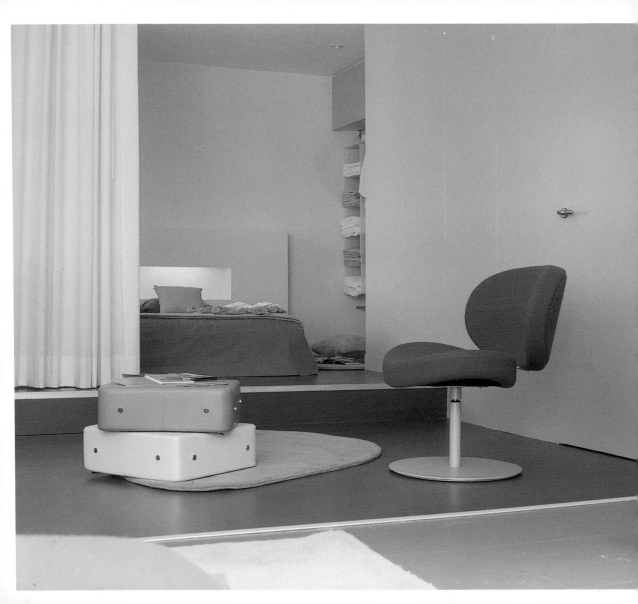

Francesc Rifé | Barcelona, Spain
Duplex in Barcelona
Barcelona, Spain | 2003

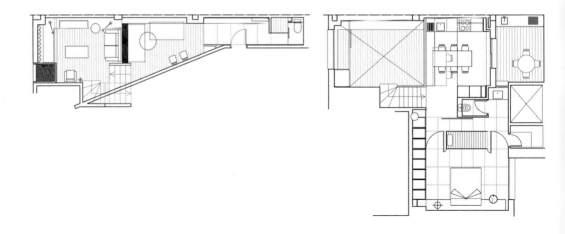

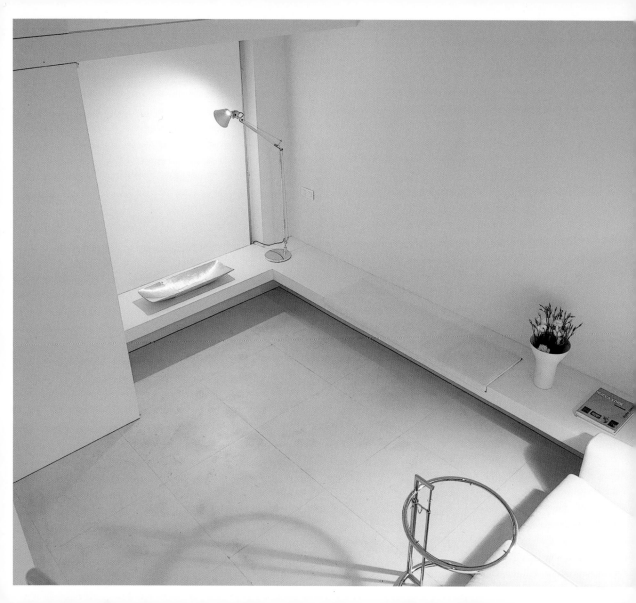

**Gabriele Buratti, Ivano Battiston, Oscar Buratti / Buratti + Battiston
Architects | Milan, Italy**
Apartamento Agnoletto
Milan, Italy | 2003

Götz Keller | Berlin, Germany
Loft in Berlin
Berlin, Germany | 2002

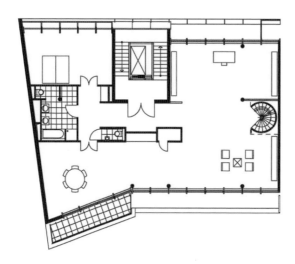

Greg Gong | Victoria, Australia
West Melbourne Warehouse
Melbourne, Australia | 2003

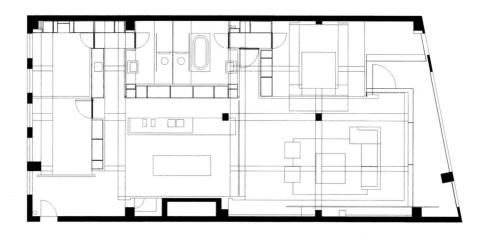

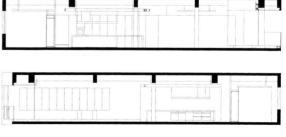

Guillermo Marín & Simona Sanchetta | Miami, USA
Italian design in Miami
Miami, USA | 2003

Guita Maleki & Pascal Cheikh Djavadi | Paris, France
Apartment in the Marais
Paris, France | 2002

Itzai Paritzki & Paola Liani | Tel Aviv, Israel
Tel Aviv 64 m²
Tel Aviv, Israel | 2003

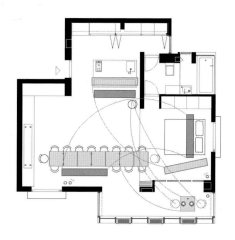
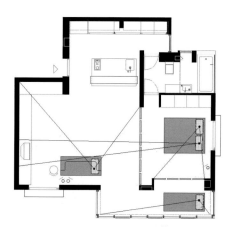

Jacquie Gray | London, UK
Apartment in London
London, UK | 2002

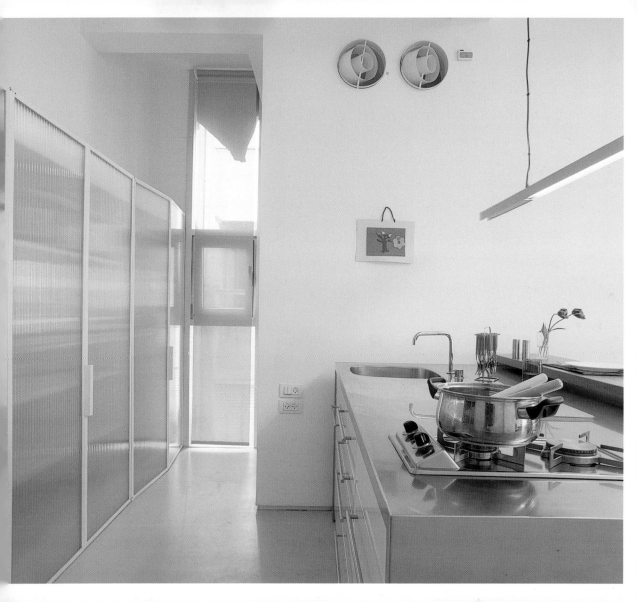

Julie Richards | London, UK
Loft in Old Street
London, UK | 2003

L.A. design & architecture studio | Paris, France
40 m² in Montparnasse
Paris, France | 2002

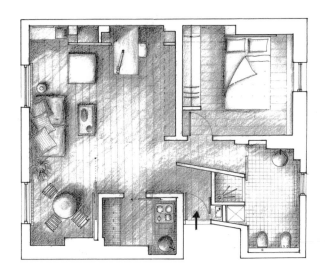

L.L. | London, UK
Industrial Loft in London
London, UK | 2003

Marble Fairbanks Architects | New York, USA

13th Street Apartment
New York, USA | 2003

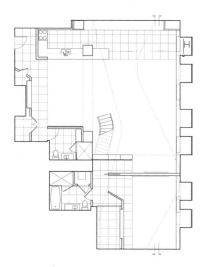
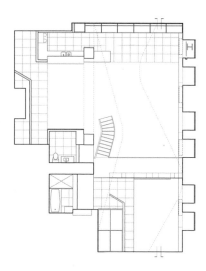

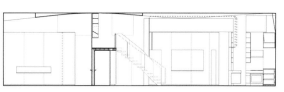

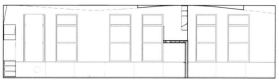

Marc Rabiner | New York, USA
Apartment in New York
New York, USA | 2003

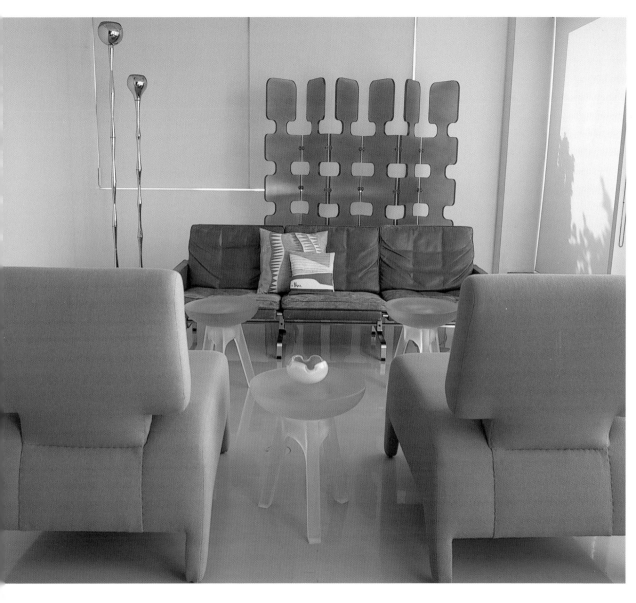

Marcelo Gizzarelli & Mercedes Sanguinetti | Bologna, Italy
Apartment in Bologna
Bologna, Italy | 2003

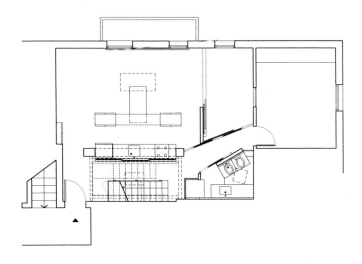

Marco Piono | Berlin, Germany
Galerie + Apartment in Berlin
Berlin, Germany | 2002

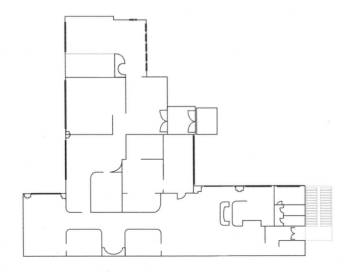

Ramón Zalabardo & Julián Barbastro | Barcelona, Spain
Apartment in Barcelona
Barcelona, Spain | 2002

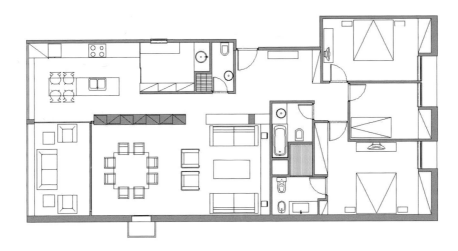

Samuel Lerch | Zürich, Switzerland
Kuessnacht
Kuessnacht, Switzerland | 2003

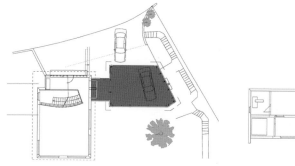
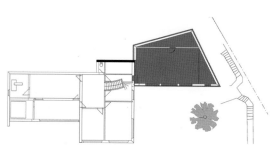

Studio Damilano | Cuneo, Italy
Casa N
Cuneo, Italy | 2003

Torsten Neeland | London, UK
Apartment in Notting Hill
London, UK | 2003

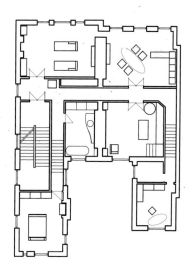

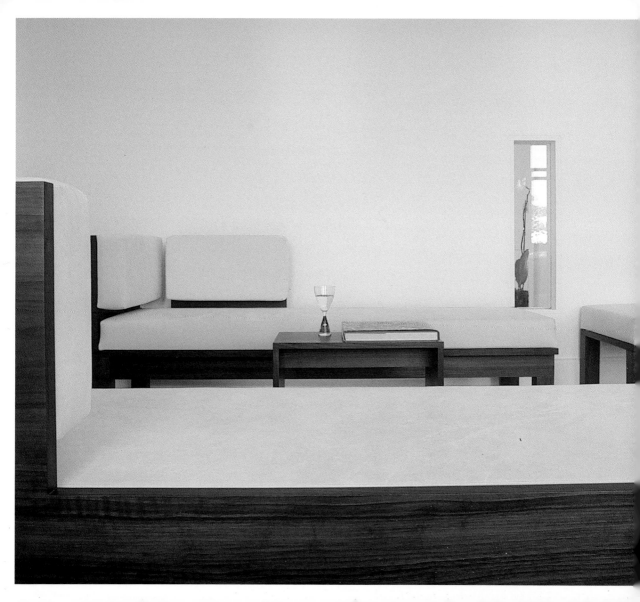

Willl Manufaktur Architektur Moebelkultur | Wien, Austria
Singlelounge in Wien
Wien, Austria | 2003

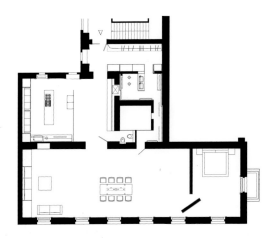

Alberto Natali Architetto
51016 Montecatini Terme (PT), Italy
P +39 (0) 572 78918
F +39 (0) 572 912693
alberto.natali@archiworld.it
Apartment in Monsummano Terme
Photos: © Alberto Ciampi

Cha & Innerhofer Architecture + Design
70 East 10th Street, Penthouse B
New York, 10003 New York, USA
mail@cha-innerhofer.com
www.cha-innerhofer.com
Green Penthouse Loft
Photos: © Dao Lou Zha

Daniele di Monte
443 española way, suite 302, Miami Beach,
33139 Florida, USA
danieledimonte@bellsouth.nct
Apartment in Miami
Photos: © Pep Escoda

Ellen Rapelius & Xavier Franquesa
C/ Brusi 18, 1°1°, 08006 Barcelona, Spain
P +34 656 44 00 80
ellen@retemail.es
Apartment in Sitges St.
Photos: © Jordi Miralles

Francesc Rifé
C/Escoles Pies 25, 08017 Barcelona, Spain
P +34 93 414 12 88
F +34 93 241 28 14
f@rife-design.com
www.rife-design.com
Duplex in Barcelona
Photos: © Eugeni Pons

**Gabriele Buratti, Ivano Battiston, Oscar Buratti /
Buratti + Battiston Architects**
20020 Busto Garolfo, Milan, Italy
P +39 (0) 331 569575
F +39 (0) 331 569063
studio@burattibattiston.it
www.burattibattiston.com
Apartamento Agnoletto
Photos: © Matteo Piazza

**Götz M. Keller /
Möritz Müller & Götz M. Keller Architekten**
Leibnitzstr. 60, 10629 Berlin, Germany
P +49 (0) 30 884 3850
F +49 (0) 30 882 4646
goetz.keller@mk-architekten.com
www.mk-architekten.com
Loft in Berlin
Photos: © Werner Huthmacher

Greg Gong
326 Tooronga Road, Malvern, 3146 Victoria, Australia
P +61 3 9822 2892
omegagg@ihug.com.au
West Melbourne Warehouse
Photos: © John Gollings

Guillermo Marín & Simona Sanchetta
Miami, USA
Italian design in Miami
Photos: © Pep Escoda

Guita Maleki & Pascal Cheikh Djavadi
110 bd. de Clichy, 75018 Paris, France
P/F + 33 1 (0) 42525364
guita.ma@wanadoo.fr
Apartment in the Marais
Photos: © Omnia-Solvi do Santos

Itzai Paritzki & Paola Liani

Tel Aviv, Israel
officepl@barak.net.il
Tel Aviv 64 m²
Photos: © Yael Pincus

Jacquie Gray, Gray Consultants

63 Earls Court Square, London SW5 9DG
P/F +44 (0) 207 2447224
JacquieGray@mac.com
Apartment in London
Photos: © Yael Pincus

Julián Barbastro / Maxilux

C/Numancia 127, 08029 Barcelona, Spain
P +34 661712053
julian.barbastro@coac.net
Apartament in Barcelona
Photos: © Jordi Miralles

Julie Richards

Unit 2, 1 Martha's Buildings, London,
EC1V 9FL, UK
P +44 (0) 20 76895095
F +44 (0) 20 76895083
julierichards@msn.com
Loft in Old Street
Photos: © Adam Butler

L.A. design & architecture studio

53, rue de Montreuil, F-75011 Paris, France
P +33 (0)1 444 99006
www.l-a-design.com
Press-director@l-a-design.com
40m² in Montparnasse
Photos: © Happyliving.DK

L.L.

London, UK
Industrial Loft in London
Photos: © Adam Butler

Marble Fairbanks Architects

66 West Broadway, suite 600, New York,
10007 New York, USA
P +1 212 2330653
F +1 212 2330654
info@marblefairbanks.com
13th Street Apartment
Photos: © Gregory Goodes Photography

Marc Rabiner

New York, USA
Loft in New York
Photos: © Reto Guntli & Agi Simoes / Zapaimages

Marcelo Gizzarelli & Mercedes Sanguinetti Architteti

Via Toffano 19, 40125 Bologna, Italy
P +39 (0) 51 6360883
gizzarelli@sanguinetti.fastwebnet.it
Apartment in Bologna
Photos: © Oscar Ferrari

Marco Piono-Visage Galerie

Gerichtstr. 12-13, 13347 Berlin, Germany
P +49 (0) 30 448 1281
F +49 (0) 30 466 07782
info@marco-piono.de
visage-galerie@snafu.de
www.marco-piono.de
www.visage-galerie.de
Galerie + apartment in Berlin
Photos: © Werner Huthmacher

Ramón Zalabardo / Rocta
Tamarit 109, 08015 Barcelona, Spain
P +34 93 426 12 02
roctascp@terra.es
Apartament in Barcelona
Photos: © Jordi Miralles

Samuel Lerch
Eibenstr. 9, 8045 Zürich, Switzerland
P +41 1 382 4655
samnad@swissonline.ch
Kuessnacht
Photos: © Bruno Helbling / Zapaimages

Studio Damilano
Via Pratolungo 1, 12100 San Rocco Castagnaretta,Cuneo, Italy
P +39 171 493504
F +39 171 493504
damilano@libero.it
Casa N
Photos: © Michele de Vita

Torsten Neeland, Industrial Design + Interior Design
61 Redchurch Street, London E2 7DJ, UK
P +44 (0) 20 77296547
F +44 (0) 20 73666583
www.torsten-neeland.co.uk
tn@torsten-neeland.co.uk
Apartment in Notting Hill
Photos: © Christoph Kicherer

Willl Manufaktur Architektur Moebelkultur
Großglobnitz 47, A-3910 Zwettl, Austria
P +43 2823 228
F +43 2823 228-19
www.willl.at
office@willl.at
Singlelounge in Wien
Photos: © Paul Ott

© 2006 daab
cologne london new york

published and distributed worldwide by
daab gmbh
friesenstr. 50
d - 50670 köln

p + 49 - 221 - 94 10 740
f + 49 - 221 - 94 10 741

mail@daab-online.com
www.daab-online.com

publisher ralf daab
rdaab@daab-online.com

creative director feyyaz
mail@feyyaz.com

editorial project by loft publications
© 2006 loft publications

editor eva dallo
layout ignasi gracia blanco
english translation ana cristina g. cañizares
french translation jean pierre layre cassou
italian translation grazia suffritti
german translation martin fischer
copy editing raquel vicente durán

printed in spain
gràfiques ibèria, spain

isbn 3-937718-17-6
d.l.   B-18673-06